DISCUSS **50**

>IT<

50 QUIZZES, CHALLENGES, AND DEEP QUESTIONS

TO GET TEENS TALKING

Standard®
PUBLISHING
Bringing The Word to Life

Cincinnati, Ohio

Published by Standard Publishing, Cincinnati, Ohio
www.standardpub.com

Copyright © Standard Publishing

All Scripture quotations are taken from the HOLY BIBLE, NEW INTERNATIONAL VERSION®.
NIV®. Copyright © 1973, 1978, 1984 by International Bible Society.
Used by permission of Zondervan. All rights reserved.

Printed in: USA
Project editor: Jim Eichenberger
Cover design: Symbology Creative

ISBN 978-0-7847-2297-8

15 13 12 11 10 09 08   9 8 7 6 5 4 3 2 1

Table of Contents

Related Lesson Themes
- Relationships with others affect relationships to God.
- We must do what we can to be peacemakers.
- Unresolved anger is destructive.

Related Bible Texts
- Proverbs 14:17
- Matthew 5:23-26
- Matthew 18:15-20
- Mark 3:1-5
- Ephesians 4:25-28

Related Lesson Themes
- The members of a healthy church build up one another.
- Christian fellowship is a partnership between those who spread the gospel.
- Joy is made complete by our relationship with other Christians.

Related Bible Texts
- Acts 2:42-47
- Acts 4:32-35
- Philippians 1:3-9
- 1 John 1:3-7

> Time on Your Hands <

Related Lesson Themes

- Setting aside time for God brings blessings.
- We must live every day as if it is our last.
- Time is a resource we must use wisely.

Related Bible Texts

- Exodus 20:8-11
- Deuteronomy 5:12-15
- 2 Corinthians 6:1, 2
- Ephesians 5:15, 16
- Hebrews 4:9-11

> Arbor-ed Emotions <

Related Lesson Themes

- God understands our feelings.
- We can come to God in the best and worst of times.
- Emotions cannot be trusted; God can be.

Related Bible Texts

- Psalm 6
- Psalm 11:1-4
- Psalm 18:1-6

> Evangelism at the Zoo <

Related Lesson Themes

- God puts people in our lives with whom we must share his love.
- Our love for others is illustrated in our willingness to tell them about Jesus.
- God wants those far from him to return to him.

Related Bible Texts

- Matthew 10
- Matthew 18:12-14
- Matthew 28:18-20
- Luke 15:8-32

> A Look at Me <

Related Lesson Themes

- God knows us best and loves us most.
- God wants us to be like Jesus and not like the rest of the world.
- God does not want us to stay the way we are.

Related Bible Texts

- Psalm 51
- Psalm 139:1-6
- Romans 12:1, 2

> Building Character <

Related Lesson Themes
- True beauty comes from good character.
- The Holy Spirit can remodel our lives from the inside out.
- Godly character can be the most effective sermon we can preach.

Related Bible Texts
- 1 Samuel 16:1-7
- Proverbs 31
- 1 Peter 3:1-8

> What Species Are You? <

Related Lesson Themes
- God hears our prayers.
- We can approach God with confidence.
- We are children of God.

Related Bible Texts
- Matthew 8:5-13
- Mark 1:40-42
- Hebrews 4:14-16

> You Are a Superhero! <

Related Lesson Themes
- Jesus wants to rescue people from this world.
- Jesus is the hero all people need.
- We are called to do Jesus' heroic work.

Related Bible Texts
- Galatians 1:3-5
- Colossians 1:10-14
- 1 Thessalonians 1:8-10
- 2 Timothy 4:18

> Your Life Story <

Related Lesson Themes
- Worship is a lifestyle.
- Worship is about God, not about us.
- God alone is worthy of our worship.

Related Bible Texts
- Psalm 95:1-7
- Psalm 96
- Psalm 100
- Revelation 5:11-14

> Would You Rather . . . ? <

Related Lesson Themes

- Pride can destroy us as well as those around us.
- Jesus showed us how to be humble.
- When we are humble, God can work with us.

Related Bible Texts

- Proverbs 11:2
- Proverbs 15:33
- Proverbs 22:4
- Philippians 2:14-16
- 1 Peter 5:5, 6

> Fear Factor <

Related Lesson Themes

- We need not be afraid when we walk with the Lord.
- Great heroes of the faith withstood evil with God's strength.
- We should respect God more than we fear others.

Related Bible Texts

- Psalm 27:1-3
- Psalm 56:1-4
- Matthew 10:26-31
- Luke 12:4-7

> What Vehicle Are You? <

Related Lesson Themes

- Even good people suffer.
- Jesus cares when we are hurting.
- God wants us to help us in our troubles.

Related Bible Texts

- Job 19:1-27
- Job 23:1-17
- Acts 4:1-30
- Acts 5:17-42

> Slogans and Submission <

Related Lesson Themes

- God's way is always better than our way.
- God places authority over us for our own good.
- Submission to legitimate authority is a sign of strength, not of weakness.

Related Bible Texts

- 1 Samuel 15:1-26
- Romans 13:1-3
- 1 Timothy 2:1-3

> Does Your Faith Have Fiber? <

Related Lesson Themes

- Jesus' miracles prove that he is who he said.
- Jesus can do the impossible.
- Jesus can heal both body and soul.

Related Bible Texts

- Mark 2:1-12
- John 11:1-46
- Acts 2:22

> Delectable Role Models <

Related Lesson Themes

- We must follow leaders who follow Jesus.
- Actions speak louder than words.
- Our behavior shapes others' views of God.

Related Bible Texts

- 1 Corinthians 11:1
- Philippians 4:9
- 1 Timothy 4:12
- Titus 2:7, 8
- 1 Peter 2:11, 12

> Where Do You Keep Your Stuff? <

Related Lesson Themes

- We are responsible to help others in need.
- God always gives us enough to share.
- God wants giving to be a joy not a duty.

Related Bible Texts

- Acts 4:36, 37
- 2 Corinthians 8:1-9
- 2 Corinthians 9:6-11

> Are You Qualified? <

Related Lesson Themes

- God has a job for each of us to do.
- We can never earn salvation.
- God equips us to serve him.

Related Bible Texts

- Luke 17:10
- Romans 3:9-18
- Ephesians 2:8-10

> Pet Piety <

Related Lesson Themes

- Our faith can allow us to take risks for God.
- We can have faith that God is faithful.
- Nothing is impossible with God.

Related Bible Texts

- Numbers 13:26-30
- Daniel 3
- Daniel 6

> Fair-Weather Friends <

Related Lesson Themes

- Loyalty is a key ingredient in relationships.
- Love is shown by our actions during tough times.
- Jesus has called us to be not only his followers, but also his friends.

Related Bible Texts

- Ruth 1
- Proverbs 17:17
- John 15:9-17

CHALLENGES

Specific calls to action in which learners are encouraged to practice specific biblical principles.

> So Much Power <

Related Lesson Themes

- The power of God is at work within us.
- God·can use even the smallest acts of kindness.
- Everything we have and are should be used in service to others.

Related Bible Texts

- Ephesians 1:18-21
- Colossians 3:23, 24
- 1 Peter 4:7-11

> The Right Clothes <

Related Lesson Themes

- Prejudice is a sin against the God who loves all human beings.
- We need to offer our friendship freely.
- God does not judge by outward appearance.

Related Bible Texts

- Acts 10:34, 35
- Romans 12:3
- James 2:1-4

> Witch or Switch? <

Related Lesson Themes

- Christianity is superior to Wicca, modern-day witchcraft.
- The Bible explains life better than does any false religion.
- Our love and God's power, not our arguments, will be effective in refuting false teaching.

Related Bible Texts

- Deuteronomy 18:9-13
- Acts 8:9-13
- Acts 19:17-20

> What Part of No Don't You Understand? <

Related Lesson Themes

- Peer pressure is powerful.
- Scripture can arm us to face peer pressure.
- God can help us withstand temptation.

Related Bible Texts

- Exodus 32:1-9, 35
- Proverbs 1:8-19
- 1 Corinthians 10:13

> Seeking Peace <

Related Lesson Themes

- Peace is more than the absence of conflict.
- God's peace is greater than the hostility of others.
- Only when we find peace with God is peace with others possible.

Related Bible Texts

- Micah 4:4, 5
- John 14:27
- Romans 5:1

> Eyes of Faith <

Related Lesson Themes

- God knows more about our troubles than we know.
- God has plans for each of us.
- We can conquer all of our troubles through Jesus.

Related Bible Texts

- Job 42:1-6
- Jeremiah 29:11
- 1 Corinthians 2:9, 10
- Romans 8:28-39

> One Foot Forward <

Related Lesson Themes

- We do not belong to the church; we are the church.
- Love is shown by our actions during tough times.
- Jesus has called us to be not only his followers, but also his friends.

Related Bible Texts

- Matthew 16:16-19
- Ephesians 3:10, 11
- 1 Timothy 3:14-16

> Video Controls <

Related Lesson Themes

- We need to think through the messages we receive from TV and in movies.
- We must guard against false teaching.
- What we believe shapes our behavior.

Related Bible Texts

- Luke 6:40
- 2 Corinthians 10:5
- Philippians 4:8

> Step Out of the Boat <

Related Lesson Themes

- Faith involves risk.
- Nothing is impossible for God.
- Jesus gives us the strength to overcome obstacles.

Related Bible Texts

- Matthew 14:22-32
- Matthew 19:26
- Philippians 4:13

> Hand in Hand <

Related Lesson Themes
- Christian unity must be our goal.
- The Holy Spirit can bring us into unity.
- The church is the body of Christ, each part supporting the other.

Related Bible Texts
- John 17:20-23
- 1 Corinthians 12:27
- Ephesians 4:3-6

DEEP QUESTIONS

Quotations, queries, and observations from sources outside of the Bible that cause learners to think more deeply about what they think about specific topics.

> Hope or Hopeless? <

Related Lesson Themes
- We can have hope in the worst of situations.
- Christians have a reason for hope when the rest of the world does not.
- All of our hopes will be fulfilled when Jesus returns.

Related Bible Texts
- Psalm 9:18
- Psalm 25:1-5
- 1 Thessalonians 4:13-18

> A Part of the Family? <

Related Lesson Themes
- The church is for everyone.
- We need one another.
- The church is unique.

Related Bible Texts
- Psalm 68:4-6
- John 1:10-13
- 1 John 3:1-3

> Rules—Who Needs Them? <

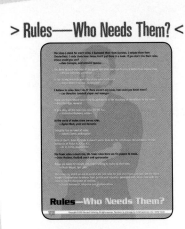

Related Lesson Themes

- God's standards are easy to understand and hard to follow without his help.
- God gives rules for our good.
- Jesus does not change God's laws but fulfills them.

Related Bible Texts

- Exodus 20
- Psalm 119
- Matthew 5:17-20

> What Is Prayer? <

Related Lesson Themes

- Prayer attunes us to God's will.
- We can pray more effectively.
- We can learn to pray by learning how Jesus prayed.

Related Bible Texts

- Matthew 6:5-13
- Matthew 7:7-12
- John 17

> How Do I Succeed? <

Related Lesson Themes

- We need to be faithful to the end.
- Don't give up on God; he didn't give up on you!
- Self-discipline is a valuable trait for the Christian.

Related Bible Texts

- Luke 18:1-8
- 2 Timothy 1:3-8
- 2 Timothy 3:10-14

> What If? <

Related Lesson Themes

- The way Jesus faced temptation made all the difference.
- Jesus' resurrection changed the world.
- Jesus' birth was a turning point in history.

Related Bible Texts

- Matthew 4:1-11
- Mark 16:1-8
- Galatians 4:4-6

> Me, a Role Model? <

Related Lesson Themes
- Who we follow shapes who we become.
- Others are looking to us for a good example.
- Not every leader is worth following.

Related Bible Texts
- 1 Corinthians 11:1
- Philippians 4:9
- 1 Timothy 4:12
- Titus 2:7, 8
- 1 Peter 2:11, 12

> Who Is Your Captain? <

Related Lesson Themes
- We cannot save ourselves.
- We must submit to God.
- Only God controls our future.

Related Bible Texts
- Acts 4:12
- James 4:13-16
- 1 Peter 5:6, 7

> Outside Looking In? <

Related Lesson Themes
- Cliques are destructive.
- We can never have too many friends.
- God seeks to bring new people into our lives.

Related Bible Texts
- Acts 9:26-28
- Romans 15:5-7
- Philemon 8-16

> Can't Wait? <

Related Lesson Themes
- For Christians, our best days are yet to come.
- Jesus' second coming should be anticipated, not dreaded.
- The prophets of the Old Testament predicted the coming of Jesus.

Related Bible Texts
- Habakkuk 3:17-19
- Matthew 24:36-51
- Acts 13:16-43

> What's the Big Deal? <

Related Lesson Themes

• Morality reflects the very nature of God.

• Obedience brings blessings.

• Disobedience brings suffering.

Related Bible Texts

• Leviticus 19:1-4

• Joshua 7

• 1 Samuel 15:1-26

> What's True? <

Related Lesson Themes

• The Bible should guide our decision-making.

• Jesus is truth in the flesh.

• The Holy Spirit guides us into all truth.

Related Bible Texts

• John 1:14-18

• John 16:12-15

• 2 Timothy 3:14-17

> How Do You Give Thanks? <

Related Lesson Themes

• Gratitude inspires sacrifice.

• We must never be too busy to give thanks.

• God can bless us more than we can imagine.

Related Bible Texts

• 1 Samuel 1:1-20

• Luke 17:11-19

• Ephesians 3:20, 21

> Whom Do You Trust? <

Related Lesson Themes

• Faith must have a secure foundation.

• We can trust Jesus for eternity.

• Love breeds trust.

Related Bible Texts

• Psalm 20:4-7

• John 14:1-4

• 1 Corinthians 13:7

> Feeling Insecure? <

Related Lesson Themes

- God knows us better than we know ourselves.
- Self-esteem is possible when we see ourselves as God sees us.
- It is what we are, not what we have, that makes us valuable.

Related Bible Texts

- Exodus 4:10-16
- 1 Corinthians 2:1-10
- 1 Timothy 6:17-21

> What Will You Leave Behind? <

Related Lesson Themes

- We need to bring the gospel to the next generation.
- Only heavenly treasure will last.
- Jesus died so we may inherit the wealth of Heaven.

Related Bible Texts

- Psalm 78:1-8
- Matthew 6:19-21
- 1 Peter 1:3-9

> What Makes a Great Parent? <

Related Lesson Themes

- God is the perfect father.
- Parents are worthy of respect.
- We are blessed when we honor godly parents.

Related Bible Texts

- Psalm 10:12-14
- Proverbs 22:6
- Ephesians 6:1-3

> Do They Know? <

Related Lesson Themes

- We are called to share the gospel.
- The gospel can be shared with a variety of methods.
- We need to be alert for opportunities to share our faith.

Related Bible Texts

- Matthew 5:13-16
- Acts 28:17-30
- 1 Peter 3:15, 16

How to Use Discuss It:
50 Quizzes, Challenges, and Deep Questions to Get Teens Talking

Discuss It: 50 Quizzes, Challenges, and Deep Questions to Get Teens Talking is a collection of 50 attractively designed discussion starters. This book contains:

• *20 Quizzes*—These quizzes are self-evaluation exercises that help teens clarify and discuss their attitudes and opinions about specific topics. You could easily start off or wrap up a session with one of these.

For example, the quiz on page 20 ("The Nature of Anger") could get your group started by talking about how they and people they know handle anger. This could lead you into a discussion of how Jesus handled anger in Mark 3:1-5.

On the other hand, the same quiz could just as effectively be used at the end of the session, challenging students to compare their own anger styles with the way Jesus handled anger.

• *10 Challenges*—These activities are specific calls to action in which students are encouraged to practice specific biblical principles. These are designed to create a powerful closing to a lesson or devotional talk.

For example, you may have a lesson on peer pressure prepared. After discussing what the Bible says about following the crowd (perhaps from Proverbs 1:8-19), you will want to give some practical direction for resisting peer pressure.

You may present the challenge from page 43 ("What Part of No Don't You Understand?"). You could brainstorm a list of specific temptations teens face. Then you may ask volunteers to role play such a situation using one of the resistance strategies listed on that page.

• *20 Deep Questions*—These pages contain quotations and queries from sources outside of the Bible that cause learners to think more deeply about what they believe about specific topics.

Each of these could be used effectively as either a session starter or an opportunity for application. "Feeling Insecure?" (page 64) could help your class open up about their self-esteem issues after reading the celebrity quotes on this page. The same page could follow a Bible study on Moses' lack of self-esteem (Exodus 4:10-16) by asking the class how Moses might address one of the celebrities cited, explaining what God taught him about self-esteem.

> Getting Started <

How you use this book is up to you. Are you unsure what you need to teach about? Browse the table of contents, which gives a full-color thumbnail image of each page along with possible lesson themes and Scripture studies for which it would be appropriate. Perhaps that will get the creative juices flowing!

Maybe you have a lesson in mind, but just need a finishing touch. Flip through the topical index or the Scripture index to find an activity that would help you present the idea or text you have in mind.

> Large group or small group? <

It really doesn't matter! Use these discussion starters for either one. For a small group, make photocopies for your students of the black and white page you need. If you like color, print full color copies from the image on the CD.

For a large group, you may use paper copies, but divide the group into smaller cells for discussion. If you want to instruct the group as a whole, project the full-color image (in .jpg format) from your laptop computer. You may also choose to imbed the image in a PowerPoint® or other projected presentation.

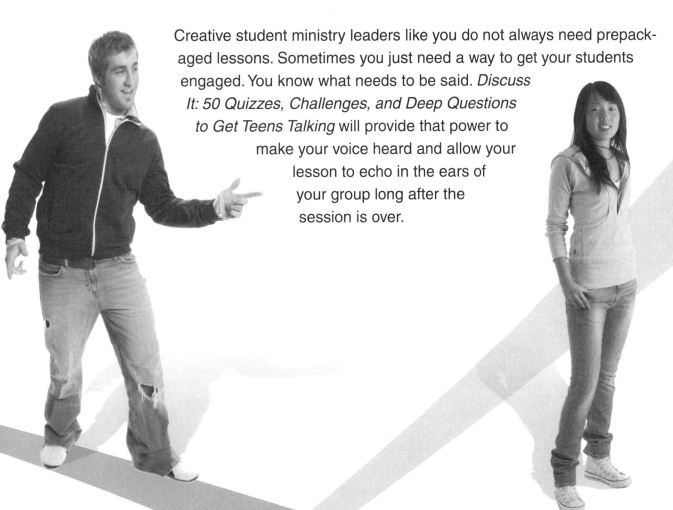

Creative student ministry leaders like you do not always need prepackaged lessons. Sometimes you just need a way to get your students engaged. You know what needs to be said. *Discuss It: 50 Quizzes, Challenges, and Deep Questions to Get Teens Talking* will provide that power to make your voice heard and allow your lesson to echo in the ears of your group long after the session is over.

The Nature of Anger

When it comes to expressing anger, which of the following describes the way you usually react? What do you need to work on to express your anger in a more healthy way?

Volcano—I hold all my anger in as long as I can, because I don't want to bother anyone. But when I can't hold back any longer, one slight thing can cause me to erupt.

Thunderstorm—When things aren't fair, I get mad. But I don't let things go too far. I make some noise and vent my feelings to people, but no damage is done.

Stream—I'm easygoing. There's not a lot that gets me flustered. I just go with the flow.

Tornado—Look out! When I'm angry, I make sure everyone knows about it. I come crashing in, stir everything up, and don't let things settle down until I get my way.

Sunlight—Don't get me wrong, I can really get heated. But it's the major stuff that really burns me, like when people are treated unjustly. I make sure my anger is used for good things though. When I get steamed, I work hard to help find a solution.

Which building below best describes your Christian fellowship? What can you do to more fully experience the type of fellowship God desires for his people?

church—Your fellowship is focused on God. Every relationship you have with fellow believers incorporates a reverence for him.

beach house—You relax together and have lots of fun with fellow believers. But nothing too deep is discussed. You just like to hang out.

office skyscraper—You feel above everyone else as if others aren't worth getting to know. People look up to you from afar but know not to get too close. Your fellowship is businesslike, only interacting when you have to or when specific tasks must be done.

cozy cottage—Your brothers and sisters in Christ feel comfortable and close with you, always right at home. They know they can drop by anytime and find you willing to listen and care.

apartment—You are surrounded by others, but you stay holed away in your area. You are too shy to get out to make new friends and connect with other Christians.

abandoned house—Keep out! You've got windows and doors nailed shut to keep people away. No one gets into your life because you've been hurt in the past and don't ever want it to happen again.

mall—You are welcoming and invite anyone and everyone to join your circle of friends. But sometimes you get a bit overwhelmed trying to please others and balance so many different requests that your friends have.

Time on Your Hands

Think about the time you spend with God each week—not just the *quantity* but the *quality*. Choose one of the timepieces below that best describes the quality of time you spend with God each week.

stopwatch—You try to squeeze in time with God when possible. But as you are praying, reading your Bible, serving other people, or spending time with him in other ways, you're always counting the minutes (and seconds!) until you can complete the task, check it off your list, and be on your way.

sundial—You soak up any time you can get with God. Spending time with him is so nice, like enjoying a sunny summer day outside. You don't worry about the amount of time you spend with him. It's not about that. It's about a relationship with someone you love spending time with. Being out in nature especially draws you to him. You spend several hours when you get the chance, just communing with your maker.

hourglass—You are regimented with your time with God. You turn the timer over, and as soon as the sand starts to trickle out, you begin your time with God. You read, pray, sing, create, serve, etc., until the sand is gone. Although this strict discipline may cause some people to see time with God as too structured, you need this regular time in your schedule to help you develop good spiritual habits. You enjoy your well-planned time and find that your ordered life has helped your relationship with God grow.

grandfather clock—Just like the dependable clock in your living room, God is always present in your life. You can call on him at any time, and you do. He is there for you, and you spend time with him throughout the day. You talk to him as you get ready for school, before mealtimes, as you are getting ready for bed at night, and lots of times in between. You don't have a set time in your schedule to read or serve or pray—it just comes naturally that by the end of the week, you've spent some good time with God.

time machine—You come to the end of each week with regret. You look back and realize that other things got in the way of your time with God. You wish you could build a time machine and go back and do things over so you could have made time with God a priority.

Arbor-ed Emotions

Think about how you typically handle your emotions. Choose one of the types of trees below that best describes how you normally deal with your emotions when overwhelming situations come your way.

weeping willow—Like a weeping willow, when people look at you, they see someone sad and drooping. Almost any stressful event causes you to cry, cry, cry. And when the tears come, they come in a flood, and it's impossible for anyone to stop them.

evergreen—Although you feel that you are being consistent—never changing like the evergreen tree—in reality, you are stuffing all your emotions away because you don't want people to see you react to anything. You think that hiding your emotions somehow makes you stronger. Yet one day you may explode with all that's suppressed inside.

cactus—Your emotions are as prickly as a cactus. No matter what life brings you, you tend to react in anger. This anger has built up over time and caused you to become a bitter person.

palm tree—As a palm tree thrives on desert islands, you deal with overwhelming situations by getting away from everyone. You don't know how to handle your emotions, so you just choose to run away and isolate yourself.

maple—Like a maple tree, you handle the seasons of life as they come. When life is rough, you feel free to express sorrow, anger, or other emotions just as a maple drops its leaves in the fall. But you don't wallow in the bad times. After a time of letting out your emotions, you blossom back into happiness like a maple's new buds emerge in the spring.

Evangelism at the Zoo

Which animal best describes your relationships with those who do not know Jesus?

a porcupine—I care, but they seem to find it hard to get close to me.

a hyena—For some reason, they think I am laughing behind their backs.

a monkey—I tend to act as much like them as possible so I can fit it. Monkey see . . .

an elephant—Anytime they offend me, I never forget it.

an owl—They seem to respect my quiet wisdom about spiritual matters.

a workhorse—I'm too busy with church activities to have time to get close to unbelievers.

a wolf—There is no room for new people in my pack of friends.

a giant tortoise—I move too slowly when I see a need and often stay in my shell.

A Look at Me . . .

If I could go on a makeover show, this is what I'd want them to fix about me:

One adjective people usually use to describe my personality:

One fear I used to have but now I've overcome:

If I were on a competitive reality show, viewers would probably notice this negative trait about me:

This is a bad habit I wish I could break:

Here's an area in my life where I need more self-confidence:

I react this way when someone gives me a compliment:

I feel like being alone when:

This was a time in my life when I felt like nobody cared about me:

Building Character

Evaluate your own inner beauty. Look at the descriptions below, and figure out which tool you need to shape your character.

Electrical plug—You need to plug into the true source of power—Jesus. You've been away from him too long, and your strength is failing. Decide to build up your strength and your character by reconnecting yourself with God.

Screws and nails—You need to mend a relationship. Your character was scarred when you had a fight with someone, and the two of you were torn apart. Decide to do what it takes to put that relationship back together.

Paintbrush—You need to brighten your spirit. Negativity has darkened your inner beauty so that it's no longer recognizable. You're starting to affect others' attitudes as well. Decide to think, act, and speak positively.

Mallet—You need to build up people instead of tearing them down. You often try to make yourself look good by making fun of other people. But it's only made you look bad. Decide to encourage others rather than insult them.

Pipe wrench—You need a firmer grasp on God's plan for your life. You generally know what Christianity is all about, but what does God want specifically with you and your abilities? Decide to seek God's guidance and wisdom.

Saw—You need to cut out a sin from your life. That sin has been controlling you and disfiguring your inner beauty. Decide to get rid of it, and don't be afraid to ask someone to help you with this process.

What Species Are You?

How do you approach God for help? Choose the animal below that describes you best.

Bunny—You're skittish; as soon as God draws close to help, you become afraid and run away.

Dog—You're loyal to God and obedient to his every command; you're always excited to be near him.

Alligator—You want to be left alone; you snap at God's attempts to reach out and help.

Butterfly—You're independent, flying wherever you want to go; you stop by to see God only when you need something.

Boa constrictor—You cling desperately to God's help; you hold on tight and don't let go!

Baby kangaroo—You're tucked close to God and dependent upon him to guide your life and provide for all of your needs; you enjoy the ride with him.

Lion—You are the king of your jungle; you reign in your own life, and you don't give up control to anyone—especially a God you can't see.

Peacock—You like to show off for God in front of others for attention; you feel it's great that God has someone as wonderful as you in His kingdom!

Sea sponge—You approach God humbly; you simply ask him to saturate you with his presence every day.

YOU ARE A SUPERHERO!

As you strive to imitate Jesus' heroic nature, try using the superhero powers you've been given from God. Which of these qualities do you possess?

- **YOU FLY FASTER THAN A SPEEDING BULLET.**
(You are quick to help people do the job, whatever is needed.)

- **YOU LEAP TALL BUILDINGS IN A SINGLE BOUND.**
(You create solutions to overcome obstacles.)

- **YOU SEE WITH SPECIAL X-RAY VISION.**
(You take time to look deep inside of people to see their true needs.)

- **YOU LIFT HEAVY OBJECTS WITH SUPERHUMAN STRENGTH.**
(You are able to pick up people who are suffering from large burdens.)

- **YOU SURVIVE BATTLES AGAINST THE ENEMY WITH A BULLETPROOF SHIELD.**
(You quickly turn to God's Word when Satan tries to trip you and others up.)

- **YOU RESCUE DAMSELS—AND OTHERS—IN DISTRESS.**
(You tell others about the saving grace of Jesus.)

- **YOU CAN HEAR A PIN DROP FROM MILES AWAY WITH EXTRA-SENSITIVE HEARING.**
(You are a great listener for many who need to talk.)

- **YOU HEAD FULL FORCE INTO THE DARKNESS WITH FEARLESS COURAGE.**
(You are not afraid to shine God's light of truth in a dark world.)

- **YOU WEAR A SUPERCOOL SUPERHERO OUTFIT.**
(You put on Jesus and allow your life to represent God to the rest of the world.)

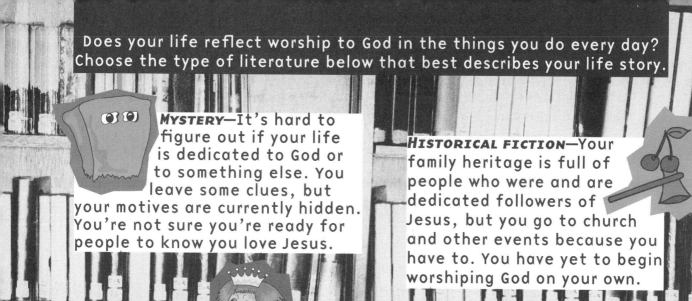

Does your life reflect worship to God in the things you do every day? Choose the type of literature below that best describes your life story.

MYSTERY—It's hard to figure out if your life is dedicated to God or to something else. You leave some clues, but your motives are currently hidden. You're not sure you're ready for people to know you love Jesus.

HISTORICAL FICTION—Your family heritage is full of people who were and are dedicated followers of Jesus, but you go to church and other events because you have to. You have yet to begin worshiping God on your own.

FAIRY TALE—Although life doesn't always have a happy ending on earth, you look forward to your eternal happy ending with God someday. Once upon a time your relationship with God began, and through its ups and downs, you've stuck with your prince and shown him lifelong dedication.

DICTIONARY—You say all the right words and go through the motions in church, but you are still searching for meaning. You wonder how Jesus fits into your daily life.

SCIENCE FICTION—When life is good, your devotion to God is out of this world! But when trouble comes, you tend to veer off into space. Sometimes it takes a major commotion to bring you back on course, but when you come back, you are sold out to God.

COMIC BOOK—Worship services are a joke to you. You think other people's devotion can be silly at times. Your life is focused solely on you—the main character.

YOUR LIFE STORY

Would You Rather . . . ?

- win a competition in which the worst singer is chosen
  OR be the first person voted off a popular reality show?

- have your team lose the game, but you personally played really great that night
  OR have your team win, but you played horribly that night?

- win every competition you enter but have no friends because you're too cocky
  OR lose most competitions but have friends who admire your humility?

- meet a big celebrity athlete and discover the person is stuck-up
  OR meet a not-so-famous athlete who's sincere and glad to meet you?

- be partners with an annoying know-it-all who tells you what to do and get an A on the project
  OR be partners with a friend and enjoy your time working but get a C on the project?

- be on a team that wins every game, but you sit on the bench
  OR be on a losing team, but you get to play the whole game, every game?

- compete against your best friend and win the prize
  OR compete against your best friend and see your best friend win the prize?

Fear Factor

This world has both evil and good in it. The evil causes all of us to fear in some way. But it's what we do with that fear that makes a difference. Read the following and choose the type of player you are in the Fear Factor game of life.

Hesitant Contestant:

You are too scared to even get involved in the game of life. You can barely watch others participate! You have so many fears that they immobilize you from living the full life that God intended.

Not by a Long Shot:

As soon as something slightly out of your comfort zone comes your way, you quickly give up. You figure it's not even worth trying to work on your fears because it's too hard.

Determined but Defeated:

Your heart races when something scares you and you're determined to try to defeat it on your own. But you end up losing your ground. You've got good intentions, but you don't realize that you'll never overcome your fears all by yourself. You need God's help.

Stunt Double:

Fear pumps up your adrenaline—as long as it's someone else's fear. You are ready to step in and help out when someone else needs assistance with fear. That's good! But you deny that you have any of your own fears to overcome.

Runner-up:

You have made some great efforts in overcoming your fears. You've given some over to God, and you're willing to let him handle them. However, there are still some you've got tucked away in hiding. You won't fully feel God's victory in this game until you place everything in his hands.

Grand Prize Winner:

You've overcome your fears and won this game! Congratulations—you placed things in God's hands and asked his help to guide you each step of the way. It was a long, hard process, but you did it. And you know that you can face whatever new fears come your way.

What Vehicle Are You?

How do react when suffering comes your way?
Choose one of the vehicles below that best describes you.

Convertible—You put the top back and go out for a drive, distracting yourself from reality by pretending the problem doesn't exist.

SUV—You don't need anyone else; after all, you have four-wheel drive, a GPS device, and all the bells and whistles possible. When problems come, you find some way to handle it on your own.

Family van—You have room for others to come near to you; you gather a group of people who love you and offer support.

Motorcycle—You zoom away, trying to outrun the problem; if you leave your current surroundings, you think your suffering may not follow.

Monster truck—You get so mad at the situation that you roll over everyone in your path, blaming others and God for your problems.

Clunker—You just break down when problems come your way, losing all ability to function; you refuse to go on until someone comes to rescue you.

Limousine—You just sit back and try to be at peace because you don't have to do all the work; God is in control, and you let him take the wheel.

SLOGANS AND SUBMISSION

Businesses use slogans to tell people about their missions and attitudes. Consider your personal attitudes and actions toward God's authority. Which one of the following slogans best describes you at this time? Which slogan would you like your life to reflect in the future?

Ford® Motor Company—Quality is Job 1.
I'm so proud of what *I* do, I may not give God any credit.

OUTBACK
Steakhouse

Outback® Steak House—No Rules, Just Right.
I like to alter God's commands to make them more "practical."

Johnson&Johnson

Johnson's® Baby Shampoo—No more tears.
I'm tired of fighting with God. I trust that he will treat me with grace.

⬤URGER KING

Burger King®—Have it your way.
I try to submit to God's commands, even when I do not understand them fully.

MCDONALDS

McDonald's®—I deserve a break today.
I think God should know I'm doing the best I can and get off my back!

International Ladies Garment Workers Union—
Look for the union label.
I know that anything good I do is because of God working in union with me.

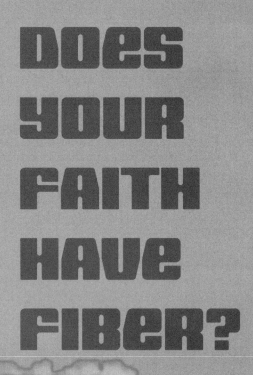

DOES YOUR FAITH HAVE FIBER?

Evaluate your faith in Jesus' miracles by choosing the breakfast cereal that best describes you.

Grits—I'll eat it if I have to. I don't question miracles or even think about them too hard. I just swallow what's put before me.

Lucky Charms®—Sure I believe in his miracles. I believe in everything—ghosts, UFOs, reincarnation . . .

Alpha-Bits®—I'll believe if someone "spells it out" for me. I want to understand why Jesus did what he did.

Granola—I have an "all-natural" religion. The idea of Jesus breaking the laws of nature is hard for me to believe.

Total®—Jesus' miracles feed my healthy faith! Knowing his power draws me to him helps me view life from his perspective and chases away my doubts.

Delectable Role Models

Are you a role model, mentor, or generally a good example to those around you? Choose one of the brand names of candy below that best describes you.

3 Musketeers® —All for one and one for all is your motto. You have listened to the wise counsel of others and put it into practice. Now you are ready to step out and be a mentor for others. You know that God's kingdom work takes a team effort of learning from some and reaching out to help others.

Snickers® —You have the talents and abilities to be a great mentor to others, but you are afraid people will laugh at you or ignore you. You have no confidence, so you never even try to put your skills to use in being a good example for someone else.

Milky Way® —Your head is out in space. You are oblivious to the needs around you. You don't even realize that you could be making a difference in someone's life by being a good example of Jesus. You are in your own little world.

PayDay® —You live your life for yourself and what you can get out of it. No one else matters. You don't care what others might think of your actions. You figure that you never asked to be a role model, so it shouldn't matter.

Butterfinger® —You try to grasp on to living a good life and being a good example for others to follow. But that goal keeps slipping out of your fingers as you fall for temptation again and again.

Rolo® —You are excited and passionate about being a role model. You try to set an example for everyone—young and old. You know you have been given certain talents that you can use for the Lord, no matter your age.

Where Do You Keep Your Stuff?

How do you handle your possessions? Choose one of the following containers that best describes your attitude toward what you own.

a sieve . . . I never get enough to satisfy. It's gone, used up, or forgotten shortly after I get it.

a safe . . . It's mine! I'm going to lock it up so nobody else can have it.

a display case . . . Look at what I've got. Look. Envy. But don't touch!

a trunk in the attic . . . I might need it someday! I hold on to a lot of things I will never use because I do not want to give them away.

a toolbox . . . If I can't use it, I don't need it. All of my possessions are practical. Nothing frilly or frivolous, please!

a wrapped gift package . . . It's mine to share, not to keep. I am willing to give what I own to someone who needs it.

ARE YOU QUALIFIED?

WHICH WOULD YOU BE MORE QUALIFIED TO DO?

become the next *American Idol* or win a million dollars on *Survivor*?

serve food at a fancy restaurant or serve food at the local soup kitchen?

win an Olympic medal or win a ribbon at the county fair?

organize a blood drive for your school or organize your closet?

become president of the United States or become president of your class?

be the lead in your school play or be the team captain for the math quiz team?

start your own online business or start a dog-walking business?

volunteer to read to kids at the library or volunteer to entertain senior citizens at a nursing home?

drive a limo for a living or drive your parents crazy?

Watchdog—I'll snarl at anyone who questions my faith, but my bark is worse than my bite.

Goldfish—I claim to love God, but he and I seem to live in totally different worlds.

Cat—I'm purr-fectly contented to lie in the sun while God takes care of me.

Horse—Sometimes I feel saddled with the burden of carrying my faith around with me.

Chameleon—My loyalty to God changes with my surroundings.

Turtle—When things get tough, I withdraw from God.

Parrot—I say all the right things, but I'm not sure I mean them.

Pet Piety

How devoted are you to God? Which of these house pets best describes your loyalty to your master?

Fair-Weather Friends

Decide which loyalty forecast below describes some specific relationships in your life. Then think of specific changes you can make to strengthen your loyalty in each relationship.

**Sunny and Hot
(loyal all the time)**

**Fair Weather
(loyal sometimes)**

**Cloudy (loyal but I
don't always show it)**

**Scattered Showers
(hardly ever loyal)**

**Continually Rainy
(never loyal)**

A friend loves at all times (Proverbs 17:17).

so much power

You may feel powerless at times, but you've got more power than you realize. How can you use your power this week?

The power of service
- plan a mission project
- send money and gifts to out-of-country missionaries
- volunteer regularly with a local organization
- reach out to others at work and school

The power of prayer
- pray daily for a friend in crisis
- pray for your classmates and teachers
- pray for church leaders
- pray for government leaders and their daily decisions

The power of a godly example
- live out your faith in front of your younger siblings
- use actions as well as words with a friend who doesn't believe in God

The power of a moral voice
- write a letter to the editor of your school paper concerning an issue
- lovingly confront a fellow Christian who is struggling with a sin

The Right Clothes

Think about people you come into contact with every day—in school, church, stores, or restaurants—both people you know and strangers.

Fine Clothes

Do you favor people who seem popular or have it all together? Maybe you want to be like them. List some of those people:

Shabby Clothes

Do you ignore people who seem out of place or different physically or mentally? Maybe you're afraid of them or don't want your reputation to be ruined by being with them. Maybe you just don't want to take the time to get to know them. List some of those people:

Love Your Neighbor

How can you change your actions toward the people you listed under Shabby Clothes? List three things you can do this month to show God's love to those people:

Witch or Switch?

The best information available indicates that the number of teens involved in Wicca is growing every year. Some of these teens become witches, even though they grew up in Christian homes.

Is the answer to become a witch or to switch some false views of Christianity they now hold? This week, look at one or more of the following concerns, and respond to the challenge of Wicca in the ways suggested.

Concern one:

Many teens, especially girls, believe that Wicca has a greater respect for women than Christianity does.

Responses: 1 Become more familiar with the stories of Ruth, Deborah, Hannah, Esther, and other strong women in the Bible.

2 Memorize **Galatians 3:28** this week, and ask God to show you how he wants you to apply it as a Christian.

Concern two:

Many teens believe that Wicca has a greater respect for protecting the environment than Christianity does.

Responses: 1 Think of these living things: a rabid dog, a rabbit that is eating the vegetables in your garden, pneumonia bacteria, a bird singing in the tree outside your window very early in the morning. Should you respond the same way to each one? Is killing one of these living things appropriate? inappropriate? Explain.

2 Write the words of **Genesis 1:26** on an index card and look at the verse regularly this week. How will this verse deepen your respect for the environment?

Concern three:

Many teens believe that Wicca's looser morality will bring them more joy than Christianity will.

Responses: 1 Take a walk on Memory Lane. Think back to a time earlier in your life when you purposely disobeyed an authority figure because you thought it would be fun. In retrospect, consider the results of that disobedience. Look for the opportunity to share that story with a non-Christian friend this week.

2 Think of a command of God that you wish would just go away! Then meditate on the words of **1 John 5:3**. Is this command as burdensome as you think? Tell God about it.

What Part of No Don't You Understand?

How can you stay strong and defend yourself against peer pressure? Here are a few things you can say to take the pressure off.

Honesty
"I don't want to."
"It's against my religious beliefs."

Rules
"If I did that, I'd be grounded for life."
"My mom and dad say I can't go."

Humor
"I'd better stay on the safe side and not lose the few brain cells I have left."
"You know, I've got to wait by the phone tonight in case (*insert cute celebrity's name here*) calls me up and asks me on a date!"

Consequences
"I could lose my spot on the team if I got caught."
"Are you kidding? We could go to jail!"

Avoidance
"I'd rather not go and be tempted to do something I shouldn't."
"I've got a better idea. How about we (*insert safe alternative plan here*)?"

What are some other ideas you've used to resist peer pressure?

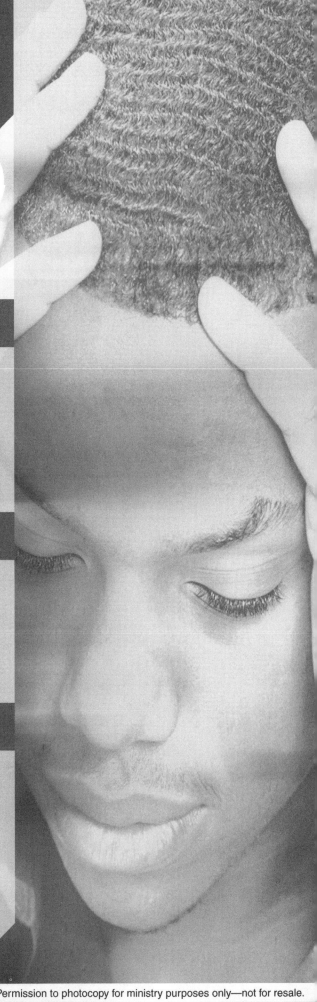

Seeking Peace

Are you experiencing the true peace Jesus offers? Consider the following:

- **Jesus gives us peace even when the world is in conflict with us.**

Thank God for his love and protection through Jesus, even when you experience troubles in life. What trials are you currently facing, either physically, emotionally, or spiritually? Allow the Scriptures to reassure you that Jesus is with you no matter what happens.

- **Jesus gives us peace by uniting all believers in him.**

Praise God for giving us brothers and sisters in Christ to encourage us, teach us, and fellowship with us. Are you currently in a conflict with a fellow Christian? If so, go to that person and do whatever you can to mend the relationship.

- **Jesus gives us peace with God by paying for our sins.**

Praise God for wanting a relationship with you and giving you a chance to draw close to him through Jesus. Is Jesus truly the Savior and Lord of your life? How can you submit your life to him more fully? Who needs to hear about this peace with God? Think of ways you can tell them about Jesus' salvation.

Eyes of Faith

Sometimes it's hard to trust in God when we don't see the full picture. When we see from God's eyes, things make a little more sense.

We may never know why we suffer. But we can be comforted that God sees more than we do. Think about a current trial you are facing. Then answer the following:

- How do you see your situation right now? What's the problem? Does it look like there ever will be a solution? How do you feel—confused, angry, hopeless, etc.?

- Try and imagine God's point of view. He knows why you are suffering. How can that bring you comfort? He already knows how your problem will be resolved. How can that give you hope?

- What good has come out of past problems you've had? How have you grown in your relationship with God and other people because of hard times? How might good come out of your current problem?

- Pray right now. Ask God questions about your problem—be honest! Tell him how you feel. Then ask for him to help you see your suffering from his point of view with eyes of faith.

One Foot Forward

God is still very active in the life of his church today. What can you do to show your love and commitment to God and his church?

Step 1: Instruction
I will actively take part in helping others follow Jesus' instructions by . . .

Step 2: Initiation
I will help others use their talents for God by . . .

Step 3: Invitation
I will strive to share the good news of Jesus with others by . . .

VIDEO CONTROLS

Read through the list below. Consider doing all or some of the following to use visual media more wisely.

○ Keep a journal of your TV and movie viewing habits for one week. Include titles of what you watched and the length of time you watched it.

○ Decide to cut your viewing time by one-tenth in the following weeks.

○ Use that one-tenth, the time you have spent in passive viewing, to actively seek God through Bible study, prayer, reading an inspirational book or magazine, or ministry activities with other Christians.

○ Look at your viewing list and mark three TV programs or movies that some might consider questionable. Pray every day for a week, asking God to direct your viewing choices.

○ Consult at least one Web site that reviews movies from a Christian perspective before choosing to rent or go to a theater to see a film. A few Web sites to consider are: http://hollywoodjesus.com, http://movieministry.com/, and http://www.cinemainfocus.com/.

○ Use the knowledge gained from one of the Web sites above to open the door to a discussion about God with a non-Christian friend.

Time after time, biblical heroes had difficulty stepping out on faith. Sometimes we have the same problem—our biggest obstacle is the fact that we doubt ourselves; we lack the confidence to keep going.

But Jesus promises to be with us no matter our doubts. Begin to work on your own confidence. Rely on Jesus and step out of the boat! Take a chance by trying one or more of the following challenges:

- Try something new—a new hobby, a new sport, a new experience—and don't worry about how well you do. Just have fun!

- Pray in the morning that God will use you to brighten the lives of everyone you see that day.

- Before you go to the next church activity, prepare yourself—get your mind ready to focus on God and your heart ready for what he has to say.

- Ask your minister a question you've always had about God or the Bible.

- Get to know someone in your church congregation from a different generation who is a mature Christian.

- Invite someone who doesn't know Jesus to a youth group activity.

- The next time a friend comes to you with a problem, pray with the person right then.

Step Out of the Boat

Hand in Hand

Plan to strengthen your fellowship with other Christians by completing one or more of the following statements:

Shake a Hand

I need to show agreement with fellow Christians, demonstrating that we are partners in sharing the gospel by:

Give a Hand

I need to shower a fellow Christian with godly applause, affirming that I want to love that person as Jesus does by:

Lend a Hand

I need to help a fellow Christian stay faithful to Christ by:

"There are no hopeless situations; there are only people who have grown hopeless about them."
—Clare Boothe Luce

"Hope is like a piece of string when you're drowning; it just isn't enough to get you out by itself."
—Robert Jordan, *The Eye of the World, Book 1*

"Until the day when God shall deign to reveal the future to man, all human wisdom is summed up in these two words—'Wait and hope.'"
—Alexandre Dumas, *The Count of Monte Cristo*

"When you reach the end of your rope, tie a knot in it and hang on."
—Thomas Jefferson

"Hope sees the invisible, feels the intangible, and achieves the impossible."
—Helen Keller

"Hope is the denial of reality."
—Margaret Weis, *Dragons of Winter Night*

Hope or Hopeless?

"They say a person needs just three things to be truly happy in this world: someone to love, something to do, and something to hope for."
—Tom Bodett

"Hope is the thing with feathers
That perches in the soul,
And sings the tune without the words
And never stops at all."
—Emily Dickinson

"All hope abandon, ye who enter here."
—Dante Alighieri, *The Divine Comedy*

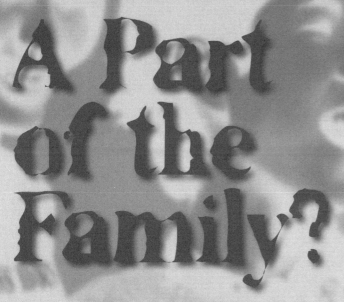

A Part of the Family?

Show how the following ideas about the family of God are false.

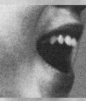
"Sure I'm involved in a church. I go every Christmas and Easter."

"I'm a part of God's family because I'm an American and God blesses America, right?"

"I go to this church because it's the place to be. I heard that anybody who's *anybody* goes here. I want to make sure I'm seen by the cool people, so I come each week."

"Service project? No thanks. I put my time in on Sunday mornings, and then I'm out of here."

"I've seen Ahmed at church. But he's from over there in the Middle East, and I just don't trust that he's a true Christian."

"My parents are members at this church, so they drag me here. I figure that's good enough—I'm covered."

The ideas I stand for aren't mine. I borrowed them from Socrates. I swiped them from Chesterfield. I stole them from Jesus. And I put them in a book. If you don't like their rules, whose would you use?
—Dale Carnegie, motivational speaker

You have to learn the rules of the game. And then you have to play it better than anyone else.
—Dianne Feinstein, politician

A few strong instincts and a few plain rules suffice us.
—Ralph Waldo Emerson, philosopher

I believe in rules. Sure I do. If there weren't any rules, how could you break them?
—Leo Durocher, baseball player and manager

There are those whose sole claim to profundity is the discovery of exceptions to the rules.
—Paul Eldridge, novelist

If you obey all the rules you miss all the fun.
—Katharine Hepburn, actress

In the world of mules there are no rules.
—Ogden Nash, poet and humorist

Integrity has no need of rules.
—Albert Camus, philosopher

Rule A: Don't. Rule A1: Rule A doesn't exist. Rule A2: Do not discuss the existence or non-existence of Rules A, A1 or A2.
—R. D. Laing, psychiatrist

The fewer rules a coach has, the fewer rules there are for players to break.
—John Madden, football coach and sportscaster

Rules are made for people who aren't willing to make up their own.
—Chuck Yeager, test pilot

The values by which we are to survive are not rules for just and unjust conduct, but are those deeper illuminations in whose light justice and injustice, good and evil, means and ends are seen in fearful sharpness of outline.
—Jacob Bronowski, historian and mathematician

Rules—Who Needs Them?

WHAT IS PRAYER?

Choose one or more of the prayers on these pages. Compare each prayer to prayers in the Bible. What elements are the same? Which are different? Which are missing? Of what significance are the differences? Is God or the person praying the main focus of the prayer? Which prayer deals most honestly with sin?

Doing the right thing is our best gift
That is what brings us bliss and happiness.
Happy and blissful is the person who does what is right,
because it is the right thing to do.
—the ashem vohu prayer · zoroastrian

Thy name is my healing, O my God,
and remembrance of Thee is my remedy.
Nearness to Thee is my hope, and love for Thee is my companion.
Thy mercy to me is my healing and my succor
in both this world and the world to come.
Thou, verily, art the All-Bountiful,
the All-Knowing,
the All-Wise.
—bahá'i prayers · bahá'u'lláh

Mother,
You are the soul of the Earth.
You are the drops of rain on a Spring Morning.
You are the cold silence of falling snow.
You envelope all life in your Life.
—gaian prayer · jason clark

I am the creator of the Universe.
I am the Father and Mother of the Universe.
Everything came from me.
Everything shall return to me.
Mind, spirit and body are my temples,
for the Self to realize in them
My Supreme Being and Becoming.
—prayer for the new age · maitreya

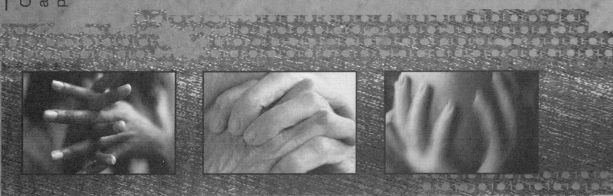

How Do I Succeed?

"You've got to get up every morning with determination if you're going to go to bed with satisfaction."

—George Horace Lorimer, former editor-in-chief of *The Saturday Evening Post*

"Nobody's a natural. You work hard to get good and then work to get better. It's hard to stay on top."

—Paul Coffey, retired National Hockey League player

"Genius is divine perseverance. Genius I cannot claim nor even extra brightness but perseverance all can have."

—Woodrow Wilson, 28th president of the U.S.

"I have an incredible perseverance in my personality . . . . That overachieving kind of drive is one of the main factors in why I made it through. I just really never give up."

—Rick Schroder, actor talking about growing up in Hollywood and not falling to problems other child actors have had

"History has demonstrated that the most notable winners usually encountered heartbreaking obstacles before they triumphed. They won because they refused to become discouraged by their defeats."

—B. C. Forbes, former author and founder of *Forbes* magazine

"The price of success is hard work, dedication to the job at hand, and the determination that whether we win or lose, we have applied the best of ourselves to the task at hand."

—Vince Lombardi, former National Football League coach most known for leading the Green Bay Packers to six conference titles and five championships

"It's always too soon to quit!"

—Norman Vincent Peale, author of many books, including *The Power of Positive Thinking* and founder of *Guideposts* magazine

"You can make a mistake by saying 'I want to be successful' or 'I want to make a lot of money.' That's the wrong goal. The right goal is 'I've got something I'm excited about, and I think I can make a difference in a unique way.'"

—Michael Dell, founder of Dell computers

"If you're a true believer, you're gonna be devoted to the ability God has given you. It's your obligation. Anything less than 100 percent is a repudiation of God's gifts."

—J. D. Drew, Major League Baseball player

"[High school] can be brutal because of the cliques and the way kids treat each other. But stick it out—it gets better. Things that seem like they mean the world at the moment, you'll look back on and realize weren't that important."

—Ben Stiller, actor

WHAT IF?

What would happen if the following people had made different choices in their moments of truth? What and who would be affected if they had done just one thing differently?

What if . . .

• Rosa Parks had chosen to stand and give up her seat on the bus?

• Christopher Columbus had sailed in another direction and reached the real India instead of the Americas?

• Eve had stepped on the snake instead of eating the fruit?

• President Truman had decided not to drop the atomic bombs on Japan in WWII?

• Theodor Geisel (a.k.a. Dr. Seuss) had chosen never to write again after his first book, *And to Think That I Saw It on Mulberry Street*, was rejected by 27 publishers?

• Brothers Dick and Mac McDonald had never sold their hamburger stand to Ray Kroc?

• Michael Jordan had quit playing basketball after being cut from his high school team?

• Fidel Castro had developed his pitching talent and pursued a career in baseball rather than becoming a dictator?

Me, a Role Model?

Read the following quotes about being or having role models.

"I want to be a good role model because it was tough to find one when I was growing up." —Chad Michael Murray, actor, *CosmoGirl*

"I'm a great role model, I give back to my community. So that makes me a good boy. The bad side is, I love to party, I have plenty of explicit lyrics. I get rid of my frustration through music. . . . I'm a good boy who makes songs about being a bad boy." —Fat Joe, rapper, *Blender*

"When you're in the public eye, it's wrong to cheat on someone, unless you're very careful. If you're normal and no one's going to know, then do it." —Paris Hilton, model/actress/singer, *Rolling Stone*

"[I returned to hip-hop] because God wanted the platform and God needed the person. I just happen to be the person that had the platform and the mouth that He could use. He needed a voice to this generation, somebody relevant." —Mase (Mason Betha), rapper/pastor, *Relevant*

"Where I grew up, you wasn't cool if you wasn't gangbangin', and I was a cool kid. There were drive-bys, I got shot at, but it was part of the neighborhood." —Omarion, singer, *Vibe*

"It's definitely harder for girls to like themselves today, with all the influences from pop culture. There are so many things they feel they have to live up to." —Lindsay Lohan, actress/singer, *CosmoGirl*

"As far as father figures, I didn't have any in my life. My mother had a lot of boyfriends. Some of 'em I didn't like; some of 'em were cool. But a lot would come and go." —Eminem, rapper/actor, *Rolling Stone*

"I was more worried about the example that major leaguers, adults, were setting for youngsters, who basically said, 'Juice up, and you'll make more money.' I believe adults have a responsibility to set good examples, particularly when you've got a spotlight on you." —President George W. Bush speaking about steroids in professional sports, *Time*

"She's my role model and my best friend. It was inevitable that we would end up facing each other in finals someday—we were both raised to believe we would be champions!" —Serena Williams, tennis star, speaking about her sister Venus, from their book *How to Play Tennis*

WHO IS YOUR CAPTAIN?

READ THIS FAMOUS POEM AND DISCUSS THESE QUESTIONS:

How is this person trying to be successful in life?

What are some consequences of trying to earn success completely on your own?

Why do you believe this poem gives comfort to some people?

INVICTUS

William Ernest Henley, 1849–1903

OUT of the night that covers me,
Black as the Pit from pole to pole,
I thank whatever gods may be
For my unconquerable soul.

In the fell clutch of circumstance
I have not winced nor cried aloud.
Under the bludgeonings of chance
My head is bloody, but unbowed.

Beyond this place of wrath and tears
Looms but the Horror of the shade,
And yet the menace of the years
Finds, and shall find, me unafraid.

It matters not how strait the gate,
How charged with punishments the scroll,
I am the master of my fate:
I am the captain of my soul.

Outside Looking In ?

"In Hollywood—much like in the average American high school—being different is not a good thing."

—Kelly Osbourne, singer

"During my teen years . . . I was awkward; I had braces; I was overweight. I was always teased. It's so funny because it's always those kids who get beaten up in school who end up triumphing. It's almost like you need that to build character—even though it's painful to go through it."

—Drew Barrymore, actress

"I got picked on growing up, and I'd be lying if I said the stuff that was said to either of us about our disabilities didn't hurt our feelings."

—Eric "Kaine" Jackson, rapper of the Ying Yang Twins, speaking about having cerebral palsy

"When I was a teenager, there were times when I felt insecure about my looks . . . At some point it dawned on me that this is the body God gave me and I have to love and appreciate it."

—Serena Williams, professional tennis player

"I think when as a girl what is communicated to you is that you have to be perfect in order to be loved, you kind of, well, at least I moved out of myself, and left a hollow being. And I filled it with anxiety and I filled it with food. Some people fill it with food or drugs or gambling or booze or shopping, but I filled it with food."

—Jane Fonda, actress

"Growing up, there were just a lot of dark things that I was angry about. That stuff started to build up inside of me. And when you hold it in, that's when you start to get into trouble—and that's what I did. I was trying to do the right thing all the time and I felt like it wasn't getting recognized. I felt like I could get attention by acting out and that then maybe somebody would listen to me."

—Ashton Kutcher, actor

"The nicknames were really cruel, and I found them utterly devastating. I don't know if I was ever well-adjusted, but I was an A student until I was about 14. Then I was bullied at school. When you're bullied, it remains a motivating factor for the rest of your life."

—Shirley Manson, singer from the band Garbage

"The day that I got chosen for the squad, I came to school and the gates of heaven opened. Everyone's opinion of me changed overnight. And it's sad. I started conforming. . . ."

—Sandra Bullock, actress, speaking about becoming a cheerleader in high school

"As a teenager, I didn't like to look in mirrors. I'd put collages and stuff over them; left the lights off in the bathroom. Those are the years when I feel like you hate yourself or love yourself."

—Christina Ricci, actress

"I'll never be happy. I believe I'll die alone. I would want it that way. I've been a loner all my life with my secrets and my pain. I'm really lost, but I'm trying to find myself."

—Mike Tyson, professional boxer

CAN'T WAIT?

They say (whoever "they" are) that anticipation is sometimes better (or worse) than the real thing. Think about the items below. What are you anticipating?

What movie, concert, or sporting event would you want to see so badly that you would spend three nights out on the street in line to get tickets?

What celebrity would you be so excited to meet that you'd make yourself sick?

What Christmas gift can you remember really wanting to get when you were little? What gift were you anticipating last Christmas?

If someone gave you $1,000, what would you most look forward to buying?

What are you most looking forward to doing when you're out of high school?

Is your anticipation about your report card being sent home usually good or bad?

Is your anticipation about going back to school in the fall exciting or sickening?

Which relative do you most look forward to visiting?

Which day do you most look forward to each year? (ex: holiday, birthday, vacation, etc.)

What task would you least look forward to? (ex: giving a speech, cleaning a toilet, etc.)

Complete this phrase: "I just can't wait until . . ."

"My whole belief in life is if it makes you happy, it's good for you."
—singer/songwriter Jason Mraz

"I must have chased a hundred girls that year, I had millions of dollars, and I went through everything too. I probably spent $100,000 a month partying."
—Wu-Tang Clan's RZA (a.k.a. Robert Diggs)

"No, not at all. There are no rules [with one-night stands]. Sometimes it can be really fun. But it can also be awful. . . . It's never really that bad. I mean, you're still sleeping with somebody, right?"
—actor Vince Vaughn

"I cuss a whole lot, but growing up, none of my brothers or I ever did drugs. We never smoked, we never drank, we never hooked up. We were good kids. But the one thing our parents let us do was cuss. They were like, 'All right, that's your one vice.' I actually think it was cool. It made us feel like our parents were edgy and that we could be honest with them."
—actress Hilarie Burton

"What's the Big Deal?"

Read these quotes from celebrities who think their actions are no big deal. But as you'll see, these things are a very big deal to followers of Jesus.

"It's not always so great to be objectified, but I don't feel I have much of a choice right now. I'm young in my career. I know I have to strike when the iron is hot."
—actress Jessica Alba

"I dabbled in cocaine, but my drug was always marijuana. And I don't see anything wrong with it."
—*American Idol* runner-up Bo Bice

"I've been clean for almost three years now. I don't do caffeine or nicotine or anything, except smoke pot."
—Mars Volta guitarist Omar Rodriguez-Lopez

"That's why I'm there. To bring smiles, even if I have to show a little cleavage."
—singer/actress Jessica Simpson

"As soon as they found out that [a drug] could be tested for, I stopped taking it. I didn't want that embarrassment, but I pushed that envelope ethically and morally because if I could take something that would help me perform better and it wasn't on the list, I was going to take it."
—former NFL player Bill Romanowski

What's True?

Read the following popular sayings. Do you agree that they are true or not? Defend your answers. How do they line up with God's truth found in Scripture?

Actions speak louder than words.

All is fair in love and war.

Cleanliness is next to godliness.

Early to bed and early to rise makes a man healthy, wealthy, and wise.

Fight fire with fire.

First come, first served.

God helps those who help themselves.

Great minds think alike.

Honesty is the best policy.

If a job's worth doing, it's worth doing well.

Let bygones be bygones.

Look out for Number One.

Look before you leap.

No pain, no gain.

Silence is golden.

The end justifies the means.

There are two sides to every question.

Time heals all wounds.

Two wrongs don't make a right.

What you don't know won't hurt you.

You don't get something for nothing.

How Do You Give Thanks?

"Thank you, thank you ever so much. I'm so happy! I love the world! I'm so happy! Thank you! . . . It's quite pretty."

Julia Roberts, Academy Award, 2001

"I accept this award in the spirit of a curator of some precious heirloom which he holds in trust for its true owners: all those to whom truth is beauty, and beauty, truth, and in whose eyes the beauty of genuine brotherhood and peace is more precious than diamonds or silver or gold. Thank you."

Martin Luther King, Jr., Nobel Prize for Peace, 1964

"For a writer of fiction to have to sit down and write a speech, especially a speech in which she must try to express her gratitude for one of the greatest honors of her life, is as difficult a task as she can face. She can no longer hide behind the printed page and let her characters speak for her. . . . What, then does she say? . . . To be a very small link in the long chain of those writers, of the men and women who led me into the expanding universe, is both an honor and a responsibility."

Madeleine l'Engle, Newbery Medal, 1963

"Today I consider myself the luckiest man on the face of this earth. I have been in ballparks for seventeen years and have never received anything but kindness and encouragement from you fans. . . . So I close in saying that I may have had a tough break, but I have an awful lot to live for."

Lou Gehrig, Major League Baseball farewell, 1939

"With a deep awareness of the responsibility conferred by your trust, I accept your nomination for the presidency of the United States. I do so with deep gratitude. . . . I'll confess that I've been a little afraid to suggest what I'm going to suggest—I'm more afraid not to—that we begin our crusade joined together in a moment of silent prayer. God bless America."

Ronald Reagan, Republican National Convention nomination, 1980

"For us, the most important task is to increase the public's right to know and to increase political transparency. This is the inescapable responsibility of Chinese news workers which is the 'force of the powerless.' As news workers, you have the right not to speak, but you do not have the right to lie. Speaking the truth is not the highest standard for news workers, but it is the bottom line. . . . I take this opportunity to call out: Please let the truth come back into our lives, and let the earth return under our feet!"

Cheng Yizhong, Guillermo Cano World Press Freedom Award, 2005

Whom Do You Trust?

The following statements were found on medical charts written by doctors:

The patient lives at home with his mother, father, and pet turtle, who is presently enrolled in day care three times a week.

The patient is a 79-year-old widow who no longer lives with her husband.

The patient refused an autopsy.

Many years ago the patient had frost-bite of the right shoe.

The patient's past medical history has been remarkably insignificant with only a 40-pound weight gain in the past three days.

Patient has chest pains if she lies on her left side for over a year.

Patient has left his white blood cells at another hospital.

The patient has been depressed ever since she began seeing me in 1983.

On the second day the knee was better, and on the third day it had completely disappeared.

She is numb from her toes down.

The patient was in his usual state of good health until his airplane ran out of gas and crashed.

The baby was delivered, the cord clamped and cut, and handed to the pediatrician, who breathed and cried immediately.

Feeling Insecure?

"Some days I would look at my reflection and see garbage. . . . But now I think I have finally reached an age where I have accepted myself for who I am."
— Shakira, singer

"My self-image, it still isn't that all right. No matter how famous I am, no matter how many people go to see my movies, I still have the idea that I'm that pale no-hoper that I used to be. . . . Tomorrow it'll be all over, then I'll have to go back to selling pens again."
— Johnny Depp, actor

"I look at myself as that same scared kid growing up trying to fit in, just trying to make it."
— Mia Hamm, professional soccer player

"When I was younger, my whole sense of self-worth was based on whether or not I was working. When I wasn't the flavor of the week, the month, or day, those were hard times."
— Kiefer Sutherland, actor

"I was 102 pounds, and people at the record label were telling me that I needed to lose weight."
— Jessica Simpson, singer

"I know I'm not ugly, but I don't think I'm a pretty girl. I'm very critical of myself, definitely."
— Drew Barrymore, actress

"I didn't have a lot of affection in my childhood, so I don't know how to be affectionate. . . . Growing up, I never heard 'I love you' from my mother, my grandmother, my father. I heard it from my mom the first time two years ago, and it still seems awkward. There's hesitance."
— Terrell Owens, NFL player

"There definitely must be an insecurity that lies beneath someone who wants to be successful and adored by other people."
— Melanie C (formerly Sporty Spice), singer

"I always feel like I'm the butler when I'm with famous people."
— Ashton Kutcher, actor

"Certainly, I was lost at times in my life. I'd like to think I was never a bad person, but I certainly went through times where I was not clear about who I was . . . where I never had a sense of purpose, never felt useful as a person."
— Angelina Jolie, actress

What Will You Leave Behind?

Can you guess each famous person who left the following provisions in his or her will?

1

. . . the Trustee is authorized to accumulate the net income . . . for health, education, support, comfortable maintenance and welfare of: (1) My daughter, Lisa Marie, and any other lawful issue I might have, (2) my grandmother, Minnie Mae, (3) my father, Vernon E., and (4) such other relatives of mine living at the time of my death who . . . are in need of emergency assistance for any of the above mentioned purposes and the Trustee is able to make such distribution without affecting the ability . . . to meet the present needs of the first three. . . .

2

I give and bequeath my "personal diaries" (as hereinafter defined) in equal shares to my daughters, Julie and Patricia. . . . If neither of my daughters survives me, I direct my executors to collect and destroy my "personal diaries." . . . At no time shall my executors be allowed to make public, publish, sell, or make available to any individual other than my executor (or except as required for Federal tax purposes) the contents or any part or all of my "personal diaries" . . .

3

I give unto my wife my second best bed with the furniture.

4

I give all of my sheet music to my son.

5

Should any child of mine be under age at the date of the death of the survivor of myself and my husband I appoint my mother and my brother Earl Spencer to be the guardians of that child and I express the wish that should I predecease my husband he will consult with my mother with regard to the upbringing education and welfare of our children.

6

I give and bequeath to my wife, Clara Mae, if she shall survive me, all my household furniture, automobiles with the appurtenances thereto, paintings, works of art, books, china, glassware, silverware, linens, household furnishings and equipment of any kind, clothing, jewelry, articles of personal wear and adornment and personal effects, excepting however . . . I give and bequeath to my Executors hereinafter named . . . all my souvenirs, mementoes, pictures, scrap-books, manuscripts, letters, athletic equipment and other personal property pertaining to baseball. . . .

1. Elvis Presley 2. President Richard Nixon 3. William Shakespeare 4. Frank Sinatra 5. Princess Diana 6. Babe Ruth

What Makes a Great Parent?

"After all these years, I have determined that it is not healthy for me to be around my father, especially now that I am responsible for my own child."

Actress Angelina Jolie, speaking of her father, actor Jon Voight

ANGELINA

"We wear each other's clothes. We wear exactly the same size in jeans."

Actress Liv Tyler, speaking of her father, Steven Tyler of Aerosmith

LIV

"The thing I owe the most to my dad is how he helped me analyze and discuss movies together. I'll never forget that."

Actor Jason Ritter, speaking of his father, actor John Ritter

JASON

"My dad never stops talking. As kids, we'd say 'Dad, Dad, Dad! Hey, Bill!' Then he'd answer."

Basketball star Luke Walton, speaking of his father, basketball star Bill Walton

LUKE

"I was on the soccer team in high school and during warm-ups I would hear, 'Run, Forrest, run!'"

Actor Colin Hanks, referring to a famous film role of his father, actor Tom Hanks

COLIN

"She just creates this energy around her that is so magnetic, you know. And with everything that she is — the most important thing [is] being a mom."

Actress Kate Hudson, speaking of her mother, actress Goldie Hawn

KATE

"I had a great deal of anger towards Dad because of his negligence and his attitude to peace and love. That peace and love never came home to me."

Musician Julian Lennon, speaking of his father, John Lennon of The Beatles

JULIAN

"My dad would have bopped me on the head when I was a kid if I came home bragging about what I did on the field. He only wanted to know what the team did."

Baseball star Ken Griffey, Jr., speaking of his father, baseball star Ken Griffey.

JUNIOR

Do They Know?

Paul took advantage of every opportunity to share the gospel with his enemies, with strangers, and with his friends. Each of us has special audiences and opportunities for which we are better suited to share our faith than any other person.

Take a few minutes to read and answer these questions. They are meant to help you evaluate how openly you share your faith with others.

1. Does your closest friend know you are a Christian?
2. Is that friend a Christian?
3. Does your closest non-Christian friend know you are a Christian?
4. Do you have any non-Christian friends?
5. Would your friends be surprised to know where you are right now?
6. Would you be comfortable explaining why you are where you are right now?
7. Would you be comfortable inviting your non-Christian friends to church? to this group? to another Bible study group or church activity?
8. Does your family share your faith?
9. Can you discuss your faith with your family?
10. Do you discuss your faith with your family and friends?
11. Do you feel confident about answering questions about your faith?
12. Do you have a plan for finding the answers you don't have? What is it?
13. Can you explain how your faith intersects with other aspects of your life? How it fits in at school? at work? in your spare time? with your family relationships? with your friendships? in your dating?
14. Do you care enough about your friends' or family's eternity to share your faith even if it means to disagree with them?
15. Do you believe that your own faith is strong enough to withstand tough questions and situations?

What Is Happiness?

"Happiness is having a large, loving, caring, close-knit family in another city."

George Burns (1896–1996)

"Happiness: a good bank account, a good cook and a good digestion."

Jean Jacques Rousseau (1712–1778)

"Life's greatest happiness is to be convinced we are loved."

Victor Hugo (1802–1885), *Les Miserables*, 1862

"The secret of happiness is to make others believe they are the cause of it."

Al Batt, in *The National Enquirer*

"True happiness is singing at the top of your lungs in your car while the people in the car next to you are staring."

Author unknown

"True happiness . . . arises, in the first place, from the enjoyment of one's self."

Joseph Addison (1672–1719)

"Happiness is your dentist telling you it won't hurt and then having him catch his hand in the drill."

Johnny Carson

"A large income is the best recipe for happiness I ever heard of."

Jane Austen (1775–1817)

"There is only one way to achieve happiness on this terrestrial ball, and that is to have either a clear conscience or none at all."

Ogden Nash

"If happiness were a food, it would be chocolate."

Author unknown

"Happiness: An agreeable sensation arising from contemplating the misery of another."

Ambrose Bierce

How Do You Face the Storms of Life?

The Bible often tells of God's power over nature. But do we believe he has that same power over the storms that happen in our lives? Sometimes that's harder to imagine.

- Do you trust God to get you through storms that happen in nature—thunderstorms, hurricanes, tornadoes, etc.?
- Do you trust God more than that, or less, to get you through the storms of life? Explain.

Think of a storm you've recently faced. Maybe it involved physical pain. Maybe it was a fight with a friend or family member. Maybe it was emotional turmoil you went through.

- Did the storm cause you to question God? If so, what questions did you ask?
- Like the disciples, did you wonder whether Jesus even cared that you were dealing with such an awful situation? How did you feel?
- How can you rely more on his power when you face your next trial?

Maybe your life is calm and peaceful right now.

- Do you still trust God with control of your life, or do you try to do it all on your own when everything is going OK?
- What steps can you take to place more control of your daily life in God's hands, rain or shine?

Scripture Index

Topic Index

True To **Life**

The *True to Life* series delivers an arsenal of studies that ring true to students and equip them to explore Bible truth in more detail. The studies are divided into three volumes that focus on the Old Testament, the New Testament, and hot topics of interest for teens and contain:

- **Real stories** – each lesson begins with a "hook," a real story about recent sports, entertainment, world news, odd events, etc.
- **Deep discussion** – each lesson has a Bible study about the topic raised in the story, complete with discussion questions and Scripture commentary for the leader.
- **Closing challenges** – students are called to action at the end of each study.

Every lesson is on a single sheet, perforated for easy removal. Plus, leaders can search the index by lesson topic, Scripture, or story. Each of the books offers a rich selection of 40 Bible lessons that are low on preparation and high in interest.

40 Instant Studies: Old Testament
Price: $9.99
Item #: 23294

40 Instant Studies: New Testament
Price: $9.99
Item #: 23295

40 Instant Studies: Bible Truths
Price: $9.99
Item #: 23296

To order, call 1-800-543-1353 or visit www.standardpub.com.

Standard®
PUBLISHING
Bringing The Word to Life